MW01042394

5 Truths About Women in Leadership

by Kelly Preston

Xulon PRESS

Table of Contents

Foreword

When it comes to the topic of women in leadership, there is no end to the wide range of opposing opinions and conflicting perspectives. Let's face it…you can get almost dizzy trying to sort out fact from fiction, what is real and true (especially from a biblical viewpoint) from what *seems* to be true only because it's been widely accepted, entrenched in hearts, and been a part of the cultural norm for so long.

That's why it's so refreshing when someone like Kelly Preston comes along and writes a clear-eyed book like *5 Truths About Women in Leadership*. Kelly deftly reveals five foundational truths that matter deeply by using compelling examples (both current-day and from secular and biblical history) of women who have led well. She also takes the time to explore and explain what the Bible has to say on this important subject, knowing that without a strong scriptural basis, the stories of influential women lack an ongoing context for those of us who long to live and lead in a God-pleasing way.

Here's the thing, though. While the content of a book like *5 Truths about Women in Leadership* is vital reading for any woman (or man) who wants to sort through the myths and misinformation to get to the heart of what women need to lead well, it is the depth of Kelly's own personal experience as a woman in ministry leadership, and her character as a Christ follower, that validates her words to me. Kelly writes from what she knows and lives. As a colleague and friend of Kelly's for the past several years, I've had the privilege of an up-close-and-personal view of her life and ministry. What I've seen makes me want to love Jesus more and love others better.

If you want to sort out fact from fiction…if you want to be inspired, challenged, and deeply encouraged about the God-given opportunities for women who take leadership seriously, this book is for you. And by applying the five truths that Kelly shares on these pages, *you*, my friend, can be a part of your own true leadership story!

Jodi Detrick, D.Min.
Author of *The Jesus-Hearted Woman: 10 Leadership Qualities for Enduring and Endearing Influence*

Acknowledgements

There is no doubt that my life has been shaped and influenced by countless people. In the last decade alone, I have especially experienced an overwhelming amount of encouragement and support to pursue God's calling. The pages in this book are inspired by those who took the time to mentor, nurture, and fan the flame of my passion to encourage women to live out their full potential for the glory of God.

I want to share my deepest gratitude to Dr. Jodi Detrick for her friendship, leadership, and for writing the foreword for this book; to the Assemblies of God Theological Seminary Women in Leadership Cohort that most definitely spurred me on, to the Ohio Ministry Network for fully supporting women in leadership, for my coaches, mentors, colleagues, and friends who have invested in me over the years.

I could not have accomplished this project without the unwavering support of my family and church family, Eastside

Community Church. Thank you for your prayers, constant encouragement, and for believing in what God wants to do in Gahanna, Ohio!

This book is dedicated to my husband and family whose love and support has been unwavering. Greg, Ricky, Claire, Jackson, Dad, Mom, Krista, Adam, Amelia, and Sofia, you are my inspiration every day! I love you and I could not have done any of this without you cheering me on!

God, my heavenly Father, this is for You! Keep me close to You always.

Introduction

"If you remain silent at this time, relief and deliverance for the Jews will arise from another place, but you and your father's family will perish. And who knows but that you have come to your royal position for such a time as this?" (Esther 4:14).

Although everyone may not have a platform to speak from, every individual has a corner of the world to influence. Where is yours? What has God entrusted to you at this time in your life?

At this time in history, people are facing trials of every kind. Yet, it is also a time of God's incredible grace. He wants everyone to hear the Good News and learn of His love for humanity. It is imperative that followers of Christ use their voices, skills, and talents to get the Word out that Jesus is real and that He loves humanity. Now, more than ever, we, as the Church, need every believer prepared and endorsed to do their part in making Christ known.

Why a book focused on women in leadership? Even though I tire of the fact that there are still opposite sides of this issue, it remains an issue, nonetheless. Some women remain hidden who genuinely desire to launch out in their God-given potential, but who do not feel authorized to carry out their mission. I get it. I had to check and double check that my role as a lead pastor was not going to hinder or go against God's Holy Word. The more I studied the Scriptures, the more convinced I became that women not only are authorized to minister and lead, but also have a biblical obligation to use their gifts and skills for the furtherance of the gospel. As women join their brothers in Christ in the work of making Christ known, their skills and talents will lead them to various roles of influence. All believers have been authorized to spread the gospel (Matthew 28:19). When God communicates a plan, nothing can stop it from being carried out. And, He does not work alone. He includes us in fulfilling His plans.

Looking back over the course of my life, I can name countless women and men who deepened my knowledge of

Christ. I know that my life would not be the same without their influence.

What about in your life? Who has inspired you personally? What if they had not been permitted to impact your life?

There is no better time to follow God's leading than at the exact moment He opens the doors. Starting a church from scratch while getting my master's degree and rearing three children, two of whom are preschool age, is probably the craziest risk I've ever taken. I couldn't have done this without the unwavering support of my husband, who also invested himself in starting this church. His belief in me and confidence in my leading role as pastor and head of this church set me up for a pretty sweet journey. I've had my own mountains to face that no one but God and I could conquer, but the role my husband has played as my partner in life and leadership has made the journey smoother.

Truth #1 Women in leadership are valuable.

"Your eyes saw my unformed body; all the days ordained for me were written in your book before one of them came to be." Psalm 139:16

Divinely Designed

Did you know that you are fearfully and wonderfully made? The love God has for you is way beyond that of any earthly parent. If God used Social Media to communicate about you, there would be never-ending posts and pictures capturing the things He loves about you! The Psalmist understood and acknowledged this remarkable attention from God: "You created my inmost being; you knit me together in my mother's womb. I praise you because I am fearfully and wonderfully made; your works are wonderful, I know that full well. My frame was not hidden from you when I was made in the secret place, when I was woven together in the depths of the earth. Your eyes saw my unformed body; all the days ordained for me were written in your book before one of them came to be. How precious to me are your thoughts, God! How vast is the sum of them! Were I to count them, they would outnumber the grains of sand—when I awake, I am still with you," (Psalm 139:14–18).

You see, God created you because He loves you. He put you together and He placed His seal of approval on you before you were born. You are His, and you belong to Him, originally. He is the One who put your heart inside of you. He watched you from before you were born, and He will see you through until the end. He gives you this great thing called, *free will* because, even though He made you, He will not force you to love Him back. Unlike humans, God does not and cannot give up on you. He made a covenant with humanity—with you (Genesis 1, 2, and 9). God breathed life into the first human—and He is still creating life. He has not stopped. He is still involved with every human being. He has not delegated this task.

From woman's debut, in Genesis 1:26–28, she was made to reflect God's image. He created both men and women in

His own image with the express purpose of revealing God to humanity. The scriptural text never suggests the inferiority of either woman or man, but rather calls for submission to God's purposes and authority. Male and female carry equal value because both are made in God's image. Genesis 2:18 describes Eve as a *helper*; this same word is used to describe God as the helper of humanity (Psalm 121). The term *helper* does not imply inferiority.

Genesis 3 breaks open the story of the Fall. Adam and Eve disobeyed God's command not to eat from the tree of life; therefore, God banished them from the paradise in which they lived. Their disobedience disrupted the balance of equality they once shared. From that time on, men and women would be tempted to try to dominate one another. The Apostle Paul, recognizing this tendency, urged husbands and wives to respect one another: "Wives submit to your own husbands as to the Lord....Husbands, love your wives, just as Christ loved the church and gave himself up for her" (Ephesians 5:22, 25). The context of these verses conveys mutual submission rather than the superiority of either partner. Therefore, men and women share equal responsibility for expressing love and respect for one another. Carole E. Becker insightfully declared that "leadership is not dominance, but rather a paradoxical combination of servanthood and authority."[1]

God, in the Garden of Eden, expressed His original intention of freedom and equality. However, with the fall of humanity and the development of patriarchal societies, these original benefits became skewed. After the Fall, society, as a whole, became patriarchal. The Bible, however, portrays women as carrying out various roles including wife, mother, public leader, businesswoman, and spiritual leader. In the midst of a male-dominated culture, God included women in His redemptive plan.

God took interest in both Adam and Eve and communicated with them both. The central purpose for each human is to have a relationship with God and to reveal Him to others. The gifts and strengths God builds into each person often lead the individual to make Him known in various capacities. God's plan is to make himself known to humanity. The bottom line is that He is looking for willing people to represent Him here on the earth. Willingness is at the top of His list of qualifications, and then He supplies the rest.

If you are willing, ask yourself how God wants to share His message of love through you. There are many messages in this world and in the church today. There is an ever-present struggle between the message of grace and the message of truth. These tensions will always exist until Jesus comes back for His Bride, the Church. A friend of mine recently asked me what I would rather my children grow up and leave home knowing: how to do things the "right" way, or that they are loved. Ideally, both, but if there was one message I could shout just a little louder than the other, it would be my intense love for each of my children. I want them to hear that loud and clear. I believe God wants us as believers to follow Him and to do what Christ did while here on earth; but more than anything else, He wants us to know without a doubt that He loves us—plain and simple. He loves us abundantly and lavishly. In fact, as Psalm 118:1 points out, God's love is never ending. It will last forever!

Whatever message is burning in your heart to share on God's behalf, let it be soaked completely in His message of love for all of humanity. "For God so loved the world that he gave his one and only Son, that whoever believes in him shall not perish but have eternal life" (John 3:16). There is no greater message of love and freedom. It is God's Holy Truth, and it is full of His unconditional grace. Whatever is said and whatever is done for the sake of making God known to this world, may it first come from a heart deeply rooted in the Father's love.

Women and men bear the image of God Almighty, and He has created in us the capacity to love others, as Jesus so beautifully demonstrated through His life of love, truth, and sacrifice. He spoke truthfully, and His message was wrapped in love. May the message we share be wrapped in His love so that the truth is not lost, and so that His grace is unhampered.

Role Models From Long Ago

I don't know about you, but I take great comfort in knowing that there are other women out there who have stepped out into leadership roles and succeeded. The following are testimonies of women who overcame incredible odds and successfully made a difference in the world. The cross section of women represented is intentional; they were not considered heroes at the time, but rather women who allowed their passion to propel their life decisions and actions. Courage and strength served as their common bond as they stepped out into uncharted waters of leadership. Leading during times of change does not come easily for anyone, but especially not for women in patriarchal societies. North American culture, now more than ever, intentionally includes women and minorities in leadership roles. More and more, women and people of varied ethnicities are being elevated and recognized for their skills and leadership talents more than for their gender or race.

Throughout history, in patriarchal societies, men assumed the primary leadership roles but looked to women for influence and wisdom. In fact, contrary to popular belief, up until the eighteenth and nineteenth centuries, women held professional and leadership roles within their communities. Women also represented their husbands in business exchanges. Some women owned and operated their own businesses. If a woman's husband died and she was able to support herself and her children through her work, she was not expected to remarry. Surprisingly, oppression and restrictions upon women arose during the Industrial Revolution in the late 1800s. The influence of women in the public sector and society as a whole diminished significantly during this era.

Let's take a look at some of the women whose leadership has inspired me. No doubt we could add to this list of incredible women, but here are a few I would like to highlight for you.

Queen Esther: Seize the Opportunity

One can learn much from women who followed their passions and dreams in the midst of great oppression. The Old

Testament records the life of Queen Esther, who exercised limited authority as a queen. In the eyes of the world, she existed merely for the pleasure of King Xerxes. However, God had chosen her for a vital role in history. Through Esther, God would save the Jews.

Esther's life started off far from palace walls; a devout Jew, she was raised by her cousin, Mordecai, some 100 years after the Jews were forced into exile in a faraway land. As a teenager, she was forcefully removed from her home and selected to become part of the Persian king, Xerxes', harem. She gained unusual favor with the king and his household. Esther stood out from the other women in the harem, and King Xerxes chose her to be the next queen.

Not long after she became queen, the Jewish people faced annihilation. Esther was faced with a choice: she could use her position for good and intervene on behalf of her people or remain in the background and not risk stepping out beyond her expected role.

Mordecai, her cousin, urged her to act: "Who knows but that you have come to royal position for such a time as this" (Esther 4:14).

Once Esther decided to get involved, she asked for an audience with the king. Though Esther held a high position, she did not have authority to make political decisions or even invite herself to speak to the king. The previous queen had disobeyed the king and been banished from society. Esther knew the risks she faced, but she chose to fast, pray, and surrender her life to God. She met with the king, revealed her true identity as a Jew, and pleaded for the lives of her people.

God was with her. The king favorably received Esther and chose not to allow the annihilation of the Jewish people. God used Esther to change history; He placed her in the right place at the right time to execute His plan.

Joan of Arc: Keep the Goal in Mind

Joan of Arc was born in 1412 during the Renaissance near the end of the Hundred Years' War between France and England. At a time when women were not soldiers, let alone commanders of armies and soldiers, God chose Joan to fight for the freedom of her country, France.[2] As a teenage girl, Joan took command of the French Army and victoriously drove the English armies from France. A woman fully devoted to God, she had known from an early age that God had chosen her for a specific mission. This mission turned out to be lifting the British siege of the city of Orleans, paving the way for

Charles VII to be crowned king of France in the city of Reims, and delivering France from England's control.[3] She achieved all of these things.

People knew Joan as an honest, pious, and fearless woman. She did not apologize for her unique purpose but gave credit to God for selecting her to deliver France. Although some people believe that French politicians used her as a means to an end before denying her validation from the French church, in her passion to see France delivered from England, she never backed down. At the age of nineteen, Joan of Arc was viciously accused of sorcery and sinning against the Mother Church of France; she was burned at the stake.[4] Her decision to obey God's calling and to fulfill His mission for her led to France's victory and her own death. Witnesses declared that Joan operated in God's strength and wisdom. Miracles surrounded her short life, and, in 1920, the Catholic Church declared Joan of Arc a hero of the faith and a saint.[5]

Pearl S. Buck: Be Yourself

In 1892, a missionary family serving in China had a baby girl, Pearl. Although her parents were missionaries, she did not grow up in a loving home. Her father did not have a high regard for women and treated his wife and family as inferior. To Pearl's father, Christian beliefs were superior to those of the Chinese culture. Consequently, he looked down on the Chinese people unless they converted to Christianity. Pearl felt alienated both culturally and physically from the Chinese children and did not have many friends growing up. She spent significant portions of time alone, either playing or writing in her journal. As an adult, Pearl began to see the Chinese through eyes very different from her father's.

As an adult, Pearl married an American missionary, John Lossing Buck. They, too, served in China. Their marriage was unhappy, and Pearl's life turned a difficult corner when her first and only child was born disabled. Through much adversity, she found her writing voice and poured herself into her novels. Her second novel, *The Good Earth*, introduced the Chinese to the Western World. Later, this book was adapted as a movie and won a Pulitzer Prize. Buck continued writing for the remainder of her life. Her literature caught the attention of the Western world; in 1938, she became the first American woman to win a Nobel Prize for literature.

Growing up in an oppressive home and then continuing to live in a Communist Society, Buck used her talents in writing to "provide both China and America telling glimpses of each other and foster exchange and understanding between the two."[6] Her choosing to use her writing gifts impacted the relationship and understanding between two powerful and dominating countries. These nations have a strong influence on the rest of the world, and Buck played a role in shaping their views of one another. In Buck's words, "The basic discovery about any people is the discovery of the relationship between its men and its women."[7] Buck bravely looked beyond the opinions and views with which she was raised to come to personal conclusions about life. She took an honest look at the Chinese people and allowed what she observed to shape her rather than simply believing what she had heard growing up.

Role Models from Not so Long Ago

Women who lived prior to the right to vote or who grew up in traditional patriarchal homes where men made all final decisions and women played a secondary role might relate to Peal S. Buck. During that era, not long ago, women only played background roles in business, government, and the church. Although known as the land of the free, the United States of America has not always been a place of freedom for all of its citizens. Until the middle of the twentieth century, men treated both African-Americans and women as subordinate. Things began to change for women during the second wave of the feminist movement in 1920, when women won the right to vote. By the mid 1960s, women had started to hold public and professional leadership roles. In the 1980s, women began to climb the corporate ladder, even starting their own companies. By the end of the twentieth century, leadership in the workplace was no longer strictly a "boys' club."

Although women were enjoying greater opportunities to serve in leadership roles in business and government, the church was reticent to follow their lead. The Church, though diverse in its beliefs, held a standard against women in leadership roles. Not all denominations hesitated to recognize and ordain women. For instance, the Assemblies of God and the Four Square Church began ordaining females early in the twentieth century. Over the years, other denominations have become more inclusive.

Sally Priesand: Do Something New

Sally Priesand, born in 1946 in Cleveland, Ohio, was raised in a Jewish family that attended a local synagogue of a Reform branch of Judaism. In her teen years, Priesand stood out as a passionate and devout adherent of the Jewish faith. She actively participated in the festivals and ceremonies at her synagogue. She shared the teachings with her friends and anyone else who would listen. Priesand took her beliefs and practices seriously and received a scholarship from her synagogue to attend the Hebrew Union College in 1964. There, her interest and passion to teach other people about the Jewish faith increased.

Although she did not want to go against tradition, she held a deep desire to become a rabbi, something never done before because people considered it sacrilegious. Once she expressed her desire to become an ordained rabbi, many people opposed her and said she could not achieve this goal. However, instead of arguing with the critics, Priesand surrounded herself with those who supported and encouraged her. She recalled, "In those days I did not think very much about being a pioneer, nor was it my intention to champion the rights of women. I just wanted to be a rabbi."[8] Priesand chose not to look at the odds stacked against her. She knew in her heart what she wanted to do and pursued her passion of leading others in her faith; in 1972, Priesand was ordained as the first female rabbi. Following her ordination, she applied for several clergy positions, but she was rejected for all of them. After several years of waiting, she became the rabbi of Temple Beth El in New Jersey. Unknowingly, Priesand opened the door for other women to serve as ordained rabbis.

Anne Beiler: When the Going Gets Tough... Keep Going

In 1949, Anne Beiler, was born in Lancaster, Pennsylvania, to an Amish family who ran their own farm. As an adult, Anne married and had children. When her youngest daughter was killed in a tragic farming accident, Anne slipped into a deep depression. She sought counsel from her pastor, but instead of finding healing and restoration, she found trouble. She had an affair with the pastor, which only plunged her deeper into depression. Later, she had another affair and ended up feeling she was squandering her life's potential. She believed that her husband and children would be better off without her, but her husband felt differently. He forgave her and loved her unconditionally through her darkest hours. After rebuilding her relationship with Christ and her family, Anne began to dream again. She and her husband moved to Texas where they lived paycheck to paycheck. One Sunday, their pastor challenged the congregation to tithe beyond their usual 10 percent. Initially, they saw this as a crazy idea, but they decided to step out in faith, believing that God would meet all of their needs. Shortly afterward, their income increased. Later, when challenged to follow Christ wherever He would lead, they moved back to Pennsylvania, and Anne became the founder of Auntie Anne's pretzel company. This company has won acclaim in the United States and around the world while demonstrating biblical standards at all levels of leadership and product development.[9]

Recently, I spoke with an Auntie Anne's employee in Columbus, Ohio. As she hand-rolled pretzels, she expressed her gratitude for working in a company whose leadership loves God and loves their employees. She handed me a children's book written about the life of their founder, Anne Beiler. She and her husband, Jonas, have made a significant difference in thousands of peoples' lives by establishing a ministry to couples and families in Pennsylvania. They have dedicated their lives to following Christ and empowering people to reaching their full potential. Anne shares openly about her experience of receiving the baptism in the Holy Spirit and how it has remarkably changed her life and ministry.

A Woman Named Refuge: Servant Leadership

While I served as a missionary in North Africa and the Middle East, I witnessed the ordination ceremony of a female pastor. This was highly unusual in this part of the world. She was ordained because she had already been pastoring and faithfully ministering to people just as other leaders who were male had. She also received official recognition for her exemplary work. She did not ask for the title of "pastor," but proved her leadership by serving as a contributing force behind the growth of the Arab Christian Church. She had actively led many Muslims to Christ and discipled them in the Christian faith. This young woman has lived up to her name by comforting people with broken hearts and lives. She gives herself fully to the work and service of the Lord because He has rescued and saved her. Every day, Refuge faces danger. Her life is threatened because of what she believes and what she does as a minister of the gospel. Though centuries removed from Queen Esther, she faces the same danger of losing her life for acting to save her people. She lives and serves in a male-dominated culture, but with humility and love for her Savior.

These women do not hail from the same backgrounds, and their lives spanned thousands of years. Nevertheless, their passion to fulfill God's mission for their lives binds them together. Only time will tell the full impact their lives have made on the world. Widening the ministry circle to include women is not intended to exclude men but rather to allow every qualified individual a voice and a place around the leadership table. We don't have to disrespectfully walk over people or push our way into leadership. When God has placed a calling on your life, He will bring it to pass. First Peter 5:6 declares, "Humble yourselves, therefore, under God's mighty hand, that he may lift you up in due time." God will faithfully accomplish His plans for humanity. Nothing can stand in His way or in the way of those He has called to serve (Isaiah 54).

Looking back over my life so far, I realize that some of my experiences have specifically shaped my calling; however, not until I understood the overarching goal of God's Word to activate every believer to make Christ known have these experiences begun to make sense. As a 14-year-old, while engaged in street evangelism in downtown Cleveland, Ohio, I remember trying to defend my faith in Christ to a Muslim man who had confronted me. The man took my Bible and opened it to a verse that I could not refute well. My default argument was to tell him about my personal experience with Jesus Christ.

Eight years later, at the age of 22, when I was a senior in college and could more adequately refute the Muslim man's argument about Christianity, I was confronted by a new challenger. My well meaning neighbor had heard that I was about to receive my ministerial credentials, and he brought his Bible over to convince me that I was out of line. He read passages from 1 Corinthians and 2 Timothy. I didn't know how to refute what he was saying, so I responded by defending my experience of God's speaking to and leading me through a series of experiences that confirmed He was calling me into ministry and leadership.

Both of these circumstances rattled me for quite some time. Although I knew my God and loved His Word, I had much to learn. I knew that I couldn't successfully navigate through the difficulties of my life's calling if my main foundation was built upon my experiences. I needed biblical proof, or else I would not be able to serve with integrity in the roles I desired. I knew that I wanted to teach and preach, but I was not willing to do these things if it was against the principles God had laid out in His Word. Rather than randomly selecting a passage of Scripture to prove the validity of our human experience, it is appropriate to consider the whole counsel of the Scriptures and

33

stand on the foundation of God's Word, biblical history, and undeniable historic precedence.

I wish I could say that my struggle was short lived, but it was not. Years later, in a seminary class when I was in my early thirties, the lights came on and freedom and liberation flooded my soul. This didn't happen after I heard a compelling speech arguing for the biblical role of women in leadership; rather, it followed my studying scripture passage after scripture passage, reading biblical testimonies, considering the entire gospel message, and reading about the cultural barriers Jesus tore down in order to reach out to and include women in His ministry. As I pictured Jesus commissioning women to spread His good news and the last-day promise and commission in which He promised the gift of His Holy Spirit to believers, the final wall of doubt came crashing down in my heart and mind. God was not calling me to lead because fewer men were stepping up to the plate; He was not calling me to be an exception to the rule. Instead, God was calling me, along with men and other women in the Body of Christ, to participate in His redemptive plan for humanity. Jesus gave His followers authorization to finish the work He had started on this earth—men *and* women waited in the upper room together for his gift of the Holy Spirit (Acts 1:4–8).

Author Carole E. Becker insightfully wrote, "A leader humbles herself to show the way. In so doing, she evokes a following."[10] Whether a woman leads an army, a political campaign, or a congregation, she bears the responsibility of being a good steward of the leadership gifts God has entrusted to her.

Truths to Remember:

Truth—I will not doubt His approval of me.

Truth—I am part of God's plan to reveal His love to humanity.

Your Turn:

1. What do you love doing?
2. What do you think your role is within the Body of Christ?

What are some of the truths that describe your life right now? As you reflect on these truths, may you be inspired to keep stepping out in faith!

Personal Truth 1:

Truth #2 Women in leadership have a job a to do.

"We are God's handiwork, created in Christ Jesus to do good works, which God prepared in advance for us to do." Ephesians 2:10

Per God's Request

While sitting in a class lecture at seminary, God asked me to shepherd His people. I thought He was asking the wrong person, but I couldn't deny the growing sense of urgency to encourage and lead people to wholeness in Christ. I spoke to my husband Greg about my desire to pastor, and he readily agreed that it was the right seat on the bus for me. He has always encouraged me to go after my dreams.

In September of 2012, together with my husband and a core team of leaders, we launched Eastside Community Church in Gahanna, Ohio. I serve as the lead pastor; Greg is the executive pastor. We are thrilled to be part of what God is doing in our community.

When we began the church-planting journey, my husband and I decided to co-pastor the church. It didn't end up working out very well because we never seemed to know who was taking the lead. After several months, we had a staff meeting (it was just the two of us then). We took a close look at our individual strengths and passions and concluded that I was better suited to the lead pastor role and Greg was better suited to the executive pastor role. This decision was an immediate blessing for both of us. We were relieved to be able to define our roles and put our efforts into developing our strengths.

Our decision to rearrange our ministry roles seemed natural and fitting. Our core team was on board 100% as well. We shared this with our spiritual leadership, the Ohio Ministry Network Executive Presbytery, and they were in agreement as well. Since our roles do not fit the traditional model, the backing of our spiritual leaders and team has encouraged us.

Our vision as pastors is to lead people to fulfill their God-given potential. We want everyone, men *and* women, to play their God-given part to reach the lost in these last days. We serve an extraordinary God who loves to be glorified through ordinary people. I'm so glad He includes us in His work!

In the last days God has promised to pour out His Spirit on both men and women, sons and daughters, old and young, slave and free. Don't be surprised by who He calls to carry His gospel message. Followers of Christ come in all types of people—a young child, an elderly person, a weary mom, an unknown and undiscovered person. Through each willing person, God desires to make himself known to the world. He will be glorified through whomever He chooses. He looks for people who want what He wants—to make Him known, to give Him glory, and to point people to the only One through whom salvation comes.

God empowers all believers to be Christ's witnesses (Acts 1:4–8; 2:17–18). Jesus' words in Matthew 28:19–20 challenge all of His followers: "Go and make disciples of all nations, baptizing them in the name of the Father and of the Son and of the Holy Spirit, and teaching them to obey everything I have commanded you. And surely I am with you always, to the very end of the age." What an impact the Church will make

39

in these final days as every available laborer launches out to fulfill his or her God-given potential. God promised to pour out His Holy Spirit on all believers to be with them in His stead (John 14:16). During His earthly ministry, Jesus began an incredible ministry of leading people to reconciliation with God the Father; now He was prepared to pass the baton to believers. He promised that believers would not be alone, but that the Holy Spirit would accompany them. This affirms God's original intention that the purpose for both males and females is to reveal God to humanity (Genesis 1 and 2).

Jesus entrusted His followers with an incredible task — building His Church. Jesus laid the foundation but gave His followers the command to build upon it by continuing His ministry. He then cautioned them not to begin the work until they had received the gift of the Holy Spirit (Luke 24:49). When this gift came, it came for all people, both male and female. God intends for every believer to put his or her faith into action by carrying out the work of reconciling humanity to God. What an exciting task for every woman and man of God to accomplish! The gift of the Holy Spirit provides the empowerment to enable every believer to succeed. The Holy Spirit gives boldness and authority to proclaim the truth about Jesus Christ (Acts 1:8) and fulfills the purpose of building the

Church. Furthermore, believers are included in the charge Paul gave to Timothy when he said, "Do not neglect your gift, which was given you through prophecy when the body of elders laid their hands on you," (1 Timothy 4:14). What talent or skill has God given you? If Paul were to address you directly today, what would he challenge you to do?

Sons and Daughters

Many women throughout the Scriptures used their God-given gifts to reach out to their communities. Miriam, the sister of Moses, was a prophetess, musician, and national leader (Numbers 12). Deborah served as a spiritual and civil leader in Israel. As a wife and mother, she also served the people of Israel as a prophetess and judge (Judges 4–5). Esther, a queen who exercised great faith, saved the Jewish people from death. Huldah ministered as a prophetess and spiritual advisor to King Josiah contemporaneously with Jeremiah and Zephaniah, other prominent prophets of that era (2 Chronicles 34:22–28). Later, the New Testament mentions Phoebe, Priscilla, Junias, Tryphena, Tryphosa, Persis, Euodia, Syntyche, and the daughters of Philip. These women confirmed the words of the prophet Joel: "I will pour out my

41

Spirit on all people. Your sons and daughters will prophesy, your old men will dream dreams, your young men will see visions. Even on my servants, both men and women, I will pour out my Spirit in those days" (Joel 2:28–29).

Jesus commanded His disciples to wait for the gift of the Holy Spirit, which they would need to carry out the ministry He began on earth (Luke 24:49). Acts 2:1–4 relays the powerful testimony of how Jesus' followers received the gift of the Holy Spirit as they waited in obedience to Christ's command. The gift of the Holy Spirit, a gift for both men and women, empowered the Church to grow (Acts 1:1–8). After the outpouring of the Holy Spirit, believers felt an urgency to spread the gospel. As they received the infilling of the Holy Spirit foretold by the prophet Joel (cf., Joel 2:29–29; Acts 2:17–21), they also were empowered to take the gospel message around the world.

Equal Opportunity Employer

The apostle Paul endorsed the leadership and ministry of Priscilla and Aquila, tentmakers like himself who frequently accompanied him on his travels (Acts 18:1–3). This couple had already converted to Christianity when Paul initially met them. He stayed in their home, which emphasizes their importance in the church at Rome (Acts 18:1–3).[11] The New Testament mentions this husband-wife team six times; contrary to the custom of the day, Priscilla's name is listed before her husband's four of the six times (Acts 18:1–3, 18, 24; Romans 16:3–4; 1 Corinthians 16:19; 2 Timothy 4:19). In a patriarchal society, a husband's name is always mentioned before his wife's. Listing Priscilla's name first could indicate her greater skill in leadership as well as her family's higher status in society. According to Ruth Hoppin, "She [Priscilla] was of an illustrious Roman family, which confirms her scholarly and cultural qualifications."[12] Gill and Cavaness believe that the prominence of Priscilla's name indicates that she played a more prominent spiritual role than did Aquila.[13] After Paul left Ephesus, Priscilla and Aquila seemed to take responsibility for the ministry (Acts 18:19). The couple mentored the eager but incompletely informed Apollos—perhaps with Priscilla taking the leading role (Acts 18:24–26)."

However, upon closer examination of this husband-wife team, neither the apostle Paul nor Luke, the author of the Book of Acts, ever indicates that Aquila held a position inferior to Pricilla's. Instead, Gill and Cavaness propose a perspective of equality: "Both women and men in the New Testament fully used all of their gifts in God's service, even if a wife's gifts might have surpassed her husband's in a certain area."[14]

Priscilla's wealthy Roman family heritage undoubtedly enabled her to be a person of learning.[15] Becoming known as a leader and teacher, she seems to have functioned in the roles of teacher, pastor, and apostle. As indicated, she spent time with a well-known and educated man named Apollos who was "mighty in the scriptures" (Acts 18:24). Apollos, likely a convert under the ministry of John the Baptist, traveled and preached the truth as far as he knew it. When Priscilla and Aquila met him, "they took him aside and explained the way of God more accurately" (v. 26) before he moved on to preach and teach in Corinth, now clearly articulating that Jesus is the Messiah. For Priscilla to have taken the lead in teaching Apollos, she clearly must have had a deep and complete understanding of the gospel.

Priscilla and Aquila—together—provided a solid ministry team and gained the apostle Paul's respect. Priscilla operated in her strengths for the sake of building the kingdom of God. She had a God-given job to do, and she succeeded within the confines of a patriarchal society. The job she did had been prepared in advance by God, just as your job has been. What if Priscilla had not taken time to instruct Apollos? What if she had not shepherded the church in Ephesus? Would the believers have missed out on what God wanted to speak through her? Absolutely!

I was once asked whether, had I decided not to fulfill my God-given assignment to write this book, God would have asked someone else to do it. My immediate answer was yes. For a long time, I've believed that if someone doesn't step out in obedience to God, then God will simply ask someone else. Perhaps in some cases that's true; however, after thinking more about it, I've changed my answer to absolutely not! God has prepared in advance specific work for you and me to do. While others may do similar jobs, they cannot do exactly what God has called you to do in the exact way that you could because they are not you. If you and I do not do the work that God prepared for us, then others will miss out. It's a simple fact. God wants to make himself known through you specifically. You have a message that is like no one else's because it's coming through your lips and your life. Are you willing to let it out?

Dream the Impossible Dream

"If God is for us, who can be against us?" (Romans 8:31). What is your dream? If dreaming has become a thing of the

past or seems like a luxury, it is time to do it again. It's not necessary to compare your dream to anyone else's; it's just important to dream big and trust the Lord. How it plays out is up to Him, but know that He wants us to pray and ask for the impossible. He is the God of the impossible, and He loves to do the impossible through ordinary people.

Truths to Remember:

Truth—I will not question God's plans.

Truth—I will listen to Him when He whispers the truth to me, even in the midst of chaos.

Your Turn:

1) Describe your God-given assignment.

2) How are you presently living out that assignment? What is another truth that describes your life right now? As you reflect on these truths (look back at chapter 1), may you be inspired to keep stepping out in faith!

Personal Truth 2:

Truth #3 The influence of women in leadership is immeasurable.

"To him who is able to do immeasurably more than all we ask or imagine, according to his power that is at work within us, to him be glory." Ephesians 3:20–21

One Sunday, I was particularly defeated after a sermon—I didn't feel good about it. I could think of a dozen reasons why it had gone wrong. This only seemed to add to the particularly tough week beforehand. I told my husband that I was discouraged and just needed to process my disappointment; then I would be fine. I went to the gym for an extra-long workout. That was helpful, but still I felt as if I were under water and drowning in defeat. I don't get as worked up over mistakes as I once did; believe me, I've come a long way. But this day had really gotten to me. I prayed;

I pushed through my bad attitude because I have a husband and family who need me to get over myself. Ha! I trusted that God would strengthen me, and He did!

That evening, I listened to several chapters in the Book of Psalms. Almost immediately, His Word washed truth and reality into the depths of my soul. I felt revived! Later that evening, my husband showed me a breakdown of how many of my sermons have been downloaded—all over the world.

Instead of feeling more pressured, I was elated. Not only was I speaking to the precious people sitting in the services on Sunday mornings at our community YMCA, I was speaking to people around the world. "God, be powerfully glorified," was my prayer. "Keep using me for Your glory, and don't let me get stuck when doubts shift my focus away from the bigger picture."

I doubt that Esther, Joan of Arc, or Pearl S. Buck had any idea just how deep an impact her life would make. In fact, I think that if you had told them how their lives would have influenced history, they might have thought you were crazy. They did not have easy lives or perfect circumstances. They endured conflict, heartache, and stress; but somehow, they managed to follow their destinies in spite of the hardships and challenges.

So did Virginia Altiere Stoffel. One of 13 children, Virginia knew conflict and hardship in every area of her life. She was put to work by the age of 13, but she worked to educate herself. In spite of the uphill climb, she kept putting one foot in front of the other, staying true to herself through heartaches, miscarriages, divorce, poverty, rejection, and the loss of loved ones. She did not stop to feel sorry for herself but instead put her energy into being a provider for her daughter and taking care of her household, at times by working several jobs. She was faithful, honest, and believed in God.

Eventually, what she had lost through suffering was redeemed in her life. Her second husband was the love of her life; she became financially blessed, and she allowed her influence to make a positive impact on her family, community, and church. She never stopped working hard, sharing her knowledge, or making sure that her legacy pointed to God.

Virginia Altiere Stoffel was my maternal grandmother. She could not have known how her choices would influence the way I was raised and the way I raise my children. She believed that with God anything is possible, and she lived out that belief. I see her influence in the lives of my mother, my sister, my father—whom she inspired on a regular basis—and my precious nieces and children.

49

It's easy to look back at the role models mentioned earlier and see that their influence likely reached far beyond their expectations. How could they have truly known the scope of God's plan and how their lives would be involved? God often reveals just one step at a time. Usually, there is no way of knowing exactly where the steps will lead. We may have a general idea of the life-long plan in mind, but it is not one hundred percent clear.

What would happen if we did know? Would we depend on God and His Spirit to lead us through, or would we run ahead and attempt to lead the way? I know exactly what I would do, and so it's better for me that God only shows me a step or two at a time. Following alongside the One who knows the way is better than navigating on my own. God is faithful.

It Matters How We Get There

In her book, *The Jesus-Hearted Woman*, Jodi Detrick points out that many women sit and wait for the doors of leadership opportunity to open for them like an elevator, when around the corner is a door to the stairs. It's not about climbing to higher positions of leadership, although that can happen; it's about taking the stairs to learning and growing as a leader rather than waiting for the perfect opportunity to fall into your lap. Detrick points out, "Stair leaders don't wait for a lucky break or the right doors to open before they serve and grow. They start where they are, with what's in front of them." Looking too far down the road can cause us to miss the opportunity we have right now.

When I was doing my graduate work, the professor would hand out the syllabus for the class, but then hold off on answering every panic-stricken question from students. Sometimes I was that student. At the time, I could not understand why my professor would not give me a direct answer but instead encouraged me to consider how to apply the project within the context of my own life. It was not that I had mean-spirited professors; it was part of their purpose to encourage each student to apply and incorporate the newly acquired knowledge in his or her own context. We were given the expectations and the tools needed but not detailed instructions. It was up to us to decide how to use the tools to fulfill the expectations.

However, I soon learned that these times were marked by vigilance and observation. The enormity of the task required me to ponder the possibilities regularly and then tune more closely into my own context. First, I had to refocus my viewing lens to pan out as far as possible, and then slowly zoom in to my corner of the world. What did God have in mind? What was He already doing around the world, and what did that have to do with where I live? Could He be wanting to do something new? If so, why would He want me, the step-by-step instruction person, to lead the change? In stepping away from our ordinary lens there is excitement, dread, and excitement. Sometimes dread wins out, too. The task is too big. The assignment far exceeds our current skills. We can rationalize away the need.

Before I became a pastor, I considered the facts: there was already a large number of churches in the community where I live, and there were already a couple of female pastors of those churches too. What did I think I was going to do that would make a significant impact anyway? It is a big community, and I only know a few people. The list of questions could go on and on. But, when God sends the invitation, the possibilities start to surface; the desire grows until the realization of the need supersedes your personal discomfort and lack of understanding. You don't need to have an answer for every question, but you must be willing to take the risk required to allow God to change your life forever. You live, breathe, and think about it all the time. You know it needs to be done. When it lines up with biblical truth, when its purpose is to save others, when it requires you to rely on God 100 percent...Houston, it's a go! It's time to launch!

The Israelites were given marching orders by God and their commander, Joshua, (Joshua 6:16–19). They had wandered for 40 years prior to entering the Promised Land. It was crucial that they all march around the city of Jericho. Rahab was in those walls, waiting to be rescued. The spies that had scouted out the city promised to spare the lives of Rahab and her family in exchange for her having hidden them from the king's soldiers.

Living as a prostitute in the land of Jericho, Rahab, most likely had limited options for pursuing other careers or dreams of her own. Talk about a lonely and hidden life! Rahab had little hope of improving her life — or so it seemed. But one day God interrupted her routine. She jumped at the chance to help the foreign spies and recognized her chance to be free from her old life (Joshua 2).

Rahab believed in God before she knew who He was. God saw her, saved her life, and chose to include her in the Israelite family. In the entire city whose destruction God had ordered, only Rahab and her family were spared — because

God had a plan and a purpose for Rahab's life. And her purpose reached beyond her life on this earth; she is part of the lineage of Christ Jesus, the Messiah and Savior of the World (Matthew 1:5). Nothing could stand in God's way. Nothing could stop His plan to rescue, redeem, and redirect Rahab's life.

Rahab did not miss the opportunity God gave her to change her circumstances because she was looking for it. She was waiting for something better and recognized it when it came. In fact, she was able to convince her family to join her as well. What if she had believed the rumors that she, along with the rest of Jericho, was doomed? What if she had believed that her life didn't matter? Had that been true, she would not have hosted the spies; she would not have survived the attack on her city, and she never would have realized her God-given potential.

What we can accomplish in our own strength is always measurable; what we can accomplish when we join with God is immeasurable! Ephesians 3:20 talks about what the Spirit of God is accomplishing in us. What is He accomplishing in your life right now? God wants to work in you so that you know Him and know how to make Him known to others. Jesus invites us to join Him and find our life's purpose in

Him. In Matthew 11:30, He says that His yoke is easy and His burden is light. This how the Message Bible puts it:

> "Are you tired? Worn out? Burned out on religion? Come to me. Get away with me and you'll recover your life. I'll show you how to take a real rest. Walk with me and work with me—watch how I do it. Learn the unforced rhythms of grace. I won't lay anything heavy or ill-fitting on you. Keep company with me and you'll learn to live freely and lightly."

What an invitation! I want to encourage you to talk to God right now. Rest or close your eyes and just focus on Him. He is already with you, and He is waiting to share good things with you. He wants to accomplish His work through your life, but He is limited when you do not go to Him. He only wishes you to carry what is tailored for your life. He wants to lift from your shoulders the non-essential burdens you are carrying right now.

No Ceiling Can Limit God's Work

The Book of Jude is short, sweet, and packed with a powerful message. Jude was fired up! He was tired of the false teaching being spread about his half-brother Jesus. He writes one of the most direct letters in the New Testament. He was defending his family, and nobody messes with family. Jude could see the bigger picture, and he reminded the believers of what it means to be focused on the goal of making Christ known in the last days. In his opening remarks, Jude says, "Relax... everything is coming together...love is on the way!" (MSG). Relax? Really Jude? How can we relax when things are, at best, chaotic in our world? Here he is not merely looking at circumstances, but he sees the end goal, God.

Not only is Jude about to give a firm reminder that Jesus is the only way to God, he is warning believers to be ready for trials, distractions, and challenges. Jude gives instructions to believers: "But you, dear friends, carefully build yourselves up in this most holy faith by praying in the Holy Spirit, staying right at the center of God's love, keeping your arms open and outstretched, ready for the mercy of our Master, Jesus Christ. This is the unending life, the *real* life!" (Jude 20–21 MSG).

Let's play this out practically. We must:

Keep our arms open wide, always receiving God's grace, knowing that we need Him. "Blessed are the poor in spirit, for theirs is the kingdom of heaven" (Matthew 5:3). The poor in spirit are those who know that they need a Savior. They continue to receive God's grace because they know that without Him *and* His grace, their efforts would be in vain. However, when we are yoked together with Christ, our efforts will not be in vain (Matthew 11:30).

Be alert. After we receive God's grace and mercy, we must be vigilant, staying above the turbulence of life around us. We all have turbulence in our lives (Ephesians 6), but our battle is not against flesh and blood. In order to achieve cruising altitude, a plane must pass through a layer of turbulence. Moving up to cruising altitude does not mean that the turbulence is no longer there; it is, but it's below the airplane. The clear blue sky is above those clouds of turbulence. Refusing to encounter that turbulence is not what makes it possible to travel smoothly but rather facing it head on and rising above it. Women and men of influence must stay on track. If they cannot see the finish line, their influence will be limited. Flying at cruising altitude allows one to see the finish line; the view is clearer and sharper. If we don't remain alert and vigilant, we risk letting the turbulence pull us down, but it's tougher to navigate below the clouds. Staying above the turbulence takes discipline; it requires receiving God's grace and mercy and staying alert.

Jude begins with the big picture, gives specific instruction, and then ends with the big picture again: "Now to him who can keep you on your feet, standing tall in his bright presence, fresh and celebrating—to our one God, our only Savior, through Jesus Christ, our Master, be glory, majesty, strength, and rule before all time, and now, and to the end of all time. Yes" (Jude 24–25 MSG). Yes! God is the only One who can keep us fresh and celebrating! Who doesn't want that? Leaders must have fresh eyes of faith to navigate through these last days.

God created humanity and birthed His purpose in each of us. His plan for redemption is fueled by His desire for humanity to know Him. He is not willing for any to perish without knowing Him. As John 3:16 reminds us, "God so loved the world that he gave his one and only Son, that whoever believes in him shall not perish but have eternal life." Let God's love for the human race be a driving factor in your leadership.

The enemy of our souls will throw every distraction in our path. As leaders, it is crucial to bear in mind that God does not oppose us; He created us. He placed His image within us and put us together. He loves us, and He is for us! When we rehearse our weaknesses and mistakes, we oppose ourselves. Nothing is wrong with knowing our weak areas—in fact, we'd better have our eyes open. The problem when we over rehearse those imperfections and focusing on weaknesses that sabotage us. When we oppose ourselves, we can thwart God's blessings in our lives. We blind ourselves to His goodness and perfection. Suddenly, we view God as imperfect, and we become offended by His ways and His thoughts. That's why He urges us to keep our eyes fixed on things above rather than on earthly things (Colossians 3:2). So much is happening in the heavenly realm that we cannot understand—so much that we cannot see, so much that we cannot put into words because they are beyond our scope or imagination. But God leads us to a greater understanding and depth of wisdom beyond what can be found in this world. Many roads lead to wisdom—humility, learning, even tragedy; but God is the only One who possesses true wisdom. And He is the only one Who can give us true wisdom.

Some people oppose women in leadership. They claim that the women mightily used in the Bible were exceptions to the rule of male leadership. They believe that women like Deborah, Huldah, and Priscilla were appointed only for a short time, and that and that women are never God's first choice for leadership. However, the book of Acts, along with the prophecy in Joel, says that in the last days God will pour out His Spirit on ALL flesh (Acts 2:17–18; Joel 2:28–29). "Sons *and daughters* will prophesy." Everyone who follows Christ must play a significant role in reconciling humanity to God. He does not want anyone to perish without knowing Him! Whether the message of truth and freedom comes from a man, woman, or child—who cares? God does! God is the One who speaks through His people and chooses whom He will to deliver His truth. We limit our own potential and that of those around us when we limit someone's role.

The overall redemptive theme throughout the Scriptures challenges the reader not to isolate specific passages pertaining to a topic and not always to settle on the literal interpretation. Rather, looking at the Scriptures as a whole and interpreting each passage while keeping in mind the original audience, cultural setting, and overall redemptive message allows a broader, more accurate perspective. William J. Webb provides great insight regarding accurate biblical interpretation: "Our task is not to lock into an ethic that has been frozen in time, but to pursue an ultimate ethic, one reflected in the redemptive spirit of Scripture."[16] Each cultural topic must be sifted through several criteria before applying it to our present culture.

First, we must consider passages such as 1 Corinthians 14:34 and 1 Timothy 2:12 within their contexts. These passages state that women are not permitted to serve in leadership roles or to exercise authority in the church. However, by bearing in mind the context in which they were written, the audience and issue addressed, and the author, one can gain a greater understanding of the purpose of these passages. In this case, the author, Paul, holds a favorable view of women serving in leadership roles. Therefore, one must consider the context of the Corinthian church and the church at Ephesus that led Paul to speak against women serving in these roles; this approach expands one's understanding of the original intent.

From a cultural point of view, both churches had women who used their influence in negative ways. They embraced false teachings about the gospel (2 Timothy 3:6) and behaved in disruptive ways during the meetings (1 Timothy 5:13). These uneducated women did not respect the spiritual authority of the church leaders. In fact, they usurped authority by spreading false doctrines. They caused significant damage to the gospel; therefore, Paul commanded that these women should not speak or hold positions of authority.

When considering these two specific passages in the midst of numerous New Testament accounts of women serving in leadership roles, one must avoid making a blanket statement for all women for all time. In the same time period when Paul was giving these specific instructions to the churches in Corinth and Ephesus, he also affirmed the ministry and leadership of women such as Phoebe, Priscilla, and Junias. Furthermore, he entrusted the leadership of the church at Ephesus to Priscilla and Aquila.

Before Paul said "I do not permit a woman to teach or to assume authority over a man; she must be quiet" (1 Timothy 2:12), he said "A woman should learn in quietness and full submission" (v. 11). Paul uses the imperative or command form of the Greek word for *should*, which indicates his radical perspective that women must learn. If God did not intend for women to lead or hold roles of authority within the church, He would only have poured out the Holy Spirit on men. However, on the Day of Pentecost, God ushered in the Church Age, which will last until Christ returns for His Church. During this period of time, God will make a final thrust to reconcile humanity to himself. In order to accomplish this task, believers who qualify and are anointed to serve in the roles of prophet, pastor, teacher, apostle, and evangelist must fully operate in their spiritual gifts.

On many occasions Jesus broke protocol with the culture. When Jesus went out of His way to meet the woman at the well (John 4), He not only broke cultural taboos by speaking to a woman in broad daylight, but He revealed his true identity to her, something He had not done before. When Jesus was resurrected, women were the first on the scene, and Jesus gave them a message to pass on to the others (Matthew 28:10). They were eyewitnesses entrusted with the most important message of all, that Jesus had conquered death!

I have heard these accounts for most of my life; I have read these passages countless times, but as I consider the fact that Christ entrusted His identity and plans to women, I am stunned. It was completely counter-cultural for Him to do so. In both the cases of the woman at the well and the women at the tomb, Jesus entrusted His message and His mission to be communicated by and carried out by women. The woman at the well took His life-changing message to her community, telling all who would listen about the One who had changed her life. The women at the tomb had a supernatural encounter with Jesus and then testified to His resurrection from the dead. It's incredibly important to understand that in those times women were not considered valid eyewitnesses. Christ alone has the ability to see past gender and look directly into one's heart. He knows those who are willing to carry his message, and He longs to reveal himself to them and launch them into action.

Whether you believe that God is making an exception to the rules of leadership for the last days or that it was always His intent to anoint and be glorified through leaders—both male and female—who will bring glory to Him, it is undeniable that God anoints women for His purposes. The last days are upon us. Our lives are not that long—70 or 80 years, on average. Imagine what could happen if we would give God our all for these precious few years here on earth. And what if we were not boxed in by traditional male and female leadership roles but rather focused on the calling and God-inspired purpose in each of our lives? The world would be changed. If what you aspire to do has never been done before, then start it so people can see it modeled in a Christ-honoring way!

What Have You Been Training For?

What circumstances have shaped your life? Since God sees our lives from the beginning to the end, and since He entrusts us to make Him known to this world, our life circumstances and spiritual disciplines play a significant role in how we are being prepared for leadership. As a young girl, I often assisted my dad in projects both indoors and out. Before a fence-building project, my dad rented a special tool called a *post-hole digger*. It consisted of two tall poles hooked together with two shovel-like scoops at the end. It looked like a giant set of tongs. After Dad used a shovel to dig a trench along the ground, he used the post-hole digger to make deep holes for the fence posts. The fence posts could then stand alone in the holes because of their depth. The purpose of the post-hole digger reminds me of the deep-rooted work that Christ does in our lives through challenging circumstances. These situations can make or break us because they are far beyond our ability to control or change, so they force us to either depend on God or walk away from Him. If we allow Him to, God will produce in us a deep-rooted work that will bring forth wisdom, perseverance, and strength of character.

Through spiritual disciplines, such as prayer, reading the Bible, spending time in His presence, and any practice that draws us closer to our Creator, He provides the means necessary for us to glorify Him. As we dig deeper in Him, He prepares us so that His glory can shine through our lives. When we align ourselves with Him, we'll see that He shares His strength and love with us in powerful ways. He moves mountains on our behalf and through our lives, even when we are unaware. *"God can do anything, you know—far more than you could ever imagine or guess or request in your wildest dreams! He does it not by pushing us around but by working within us, his Spirit deeply and gently within us. Glory to God in the church! Glory to God in the Messiah, in Jesus! Glory down all the generations! Glory through all millennia! Oh, yes!" (Ephesians 3:20–21, MSG).*

Truths to Remember:

Truth—What I do in my own strength is measurable, what God does through my life is immeasurable.

Truth—He is influencing others through my life right now.

Your Turn:

    1) What have you been training for? (Take a moment to consider the circumstances that have shaped your life.

Also, what spiritual disciplines do you practice and how do they draw you closer to God?)

2) How can you deepen your connection with Christ today? This week? This month?

What is another truth that describes your life right now? As you reflect on these truths (look back at chapters 1 & 2), may you be inspired to keep stepping out in faith!

Personal Truth 3:

Truth #4 Women in leadership are courageous.

"The Spirit God gave us does not make us timid, but gives us power, love and self-discipline." 2 Timothy 1:7

Don't Let Fear Be Your Excuse

"She believed she could, so she did." That's what the plaque on my desk says. I look at it routinely, and it brings a smile to my face. A few times I've scoffed at it when I've felt defeated. Tucked inside the back of the plaque is a handwritten note from my sister, Krista Scheetz. I believe this message is for you too:

"I am proud of you for taking risks—for not settling—for wanting and asking for more

*out of life! Keep living your life out loud—
embracing the messy with the neat! You
have so much wisdom, love, and insight to
share. We need to hear your story! You are a
hero to me!"*

Everyone needs a cheerleader—someone who believes in her and tells her so. I'm cheering for you right now. Be encouraged that you are needed and that your story is important! Pursuing a dream can be downright scary, but having someone spur you on in the process can be a lifesaver.

One of the greatest roadblocks to overcoming fear is fear. If we cultivate fear, it can become a deadly disease coursing through our veins. It will cause us to stop, to procrastinate, to pass up opportunities, and to stay on standby mode for the rest of our lives. Paul knew that fear would prevent his young friend Timothy from reaching his full potential; this is why he admonished Timothy, his spiritual son, not to be afraid of being a young leader in his ministry position but to focus on who he was in Christ (2 Timothy 1:7). If Timothy had backed away from the opportunity to minister to God's people out of fear, he would not have utilized his spiritual or natural gifts in the way God intended.

One of Satan's most prevalent tactics focuses on instilling fear in Christ's followers. By influencing fear-based decisions, Satan can have a hand in thwarting God's redemptive plan for humanity. However, God's children are perfected in His love: "Perfect love casts out fear" (1 John 4:18, NASB). God is the personification of love, and the tasks He assigns to His children are motivated by His love for humanity. We see this again in John 3:16: "God so loved the world that he gave his one and only Son, that whoever believes in him shall not perish but have eternal life." More than just a sentimental statement, this truth serves as the driving force behind all of God's actions and His ultimate plan.

Relinquish Control

A second critical component to overcoming fear is letting go of control. Don't confuse this with abandoning self-control; this is about letting go of the need to control the people and circumstances in your life. Leaders are taught and trained to be in control and to be prepared for the unexpected. While this is important, it can be taken to extremes. Leaders who try to control everything will burn out. They'll also cause others to stop following them. Surely you know such an ultra-micromanagers—maybe it's even you.

One of the greatest leadership lessons I learned under a former mentor and boss was to let others shine and have the spot light as often as possible. He would routinely and intentionally give others the big opportunities to represent the whole team. He cheered them on and pushed them out of the nest in a way similar to a mother bird's forcing her chicks to learn to fly. Sometimes it didn't make sense to me; it seemed that he, as the top leader, should reserve for himself all of the important opportunities to represent the ministry and the team, but he regularly pushed others out into the spotlight. He loved to watch them find their wings! As a result, he fostered trust and tremendous momentum on the team.

Before the stair exercise machine in the gym at my local YMCA, there is a mat on the floor in front of the machine that reads, "Control Zone." Once you select "go," The steps begin to come down one at a time at a consistent pace. There's no slowing down unless you manually adjust the settings on the control panel. After my first time using the stair machine, I noticed that I had climbed higher than I would have on my own because I was keeping the machine's set pace; I just had to keep putting one foot in front of the other and hold on to the sidebars. By the end of my workout, I had climbed more than 800 steps! I never would have accomplished that if the steps had been outside a tall building. I would have walked on by. But on the machine, it was easier to climb that high because I just had to keep taking one step at a time. My responsibility was to stay on and keep my legs moving, and the machine did the rest. The mat labeled, "Control Zone," is accurately worded. Though the participant decides the speed and height of the climb, the machine will not stop until the goal is achieved.

While I'm at the gym, I usually observe others using the stair machine. Some look like I do; they keep pace but look tired. Others make it look like they are under-challenged; they take two steps at a time without holding on to the rails. They can do this for long periods of time, too! It can be intimidating to use the machine next to a pro like that. It can feel as if everyone in the gym is judging your performance. My fear is temporary though, because once I'm climbing the stairs, my only concern is to meet each step and not fall off. Eventually, I get caught up in my own workout, and I'm no longer thinking about the pro next to me or wondering whether others are watching how I do it. It doesn't matter how I look while I am on the machine, how graceful or strong I appear, but it does matter that I start and finish the workout. If I let fear get in the way, I would never get on the machine or know the satisfaction of conquering all those stairs.

How many times do we put things off or minimize the prompting of the Holy Spirit because it would mean stepping out of the control zone and into the unknown. I'm not just talking about life-changing opportunities either; just a simple change in our daily routine might be all it takes to say yes to following the leading of the Lord to do something that we normally wouldn't have done. It may not look graceful, and we may not look like a pro doing it, but we'll be exercising faith. God looks for those who are willing to step out of their control zones and exercise their faith one step at a time. The courage we need to step out—and stay out there—in the face of challenges and challengers will arise from our security in Christ's calling and assignment. We need no approval other than His, and at the end of the day, if we have done what He has asked of us, then fear and faith have collided, and faith won.

Letting go of control can also mean harnessing our control-freak tendencies. One of the surest ways to tame our control-freak nature is to open ourselves up to feedback. This is both a pride crusher and a lifesaver. In *Boundaries for Leaders* Dr. Henry Cloud applauds this principle from Ken Blanchard,

"Feedback is the breakfast of champions." Feedback is good. We need to hear how we're doing on a regular basis. Wisdom accepts feedback as a gift; foolishness perceives it as a threat. Psalm 111.10 reminds us, "The fear of the LORD is the beginning of wisdom." That kind of fear means being surrendered to God, listening to and waiting on Him. If we are anchored in God, then feedback will propel us to our destiny rather than derailing our plans. Feedback is our friend. As we draw close to God, He gives us discernment to recognize unhelpful feedback that would harm His plans. As a woman leader, I sometimes wonder if there isn't additional pressure to perform with excellence at all times. I have heard women confess that they experience added pressure as leaders, not only because of their role but also because of their gender. If they make a mistake as a leader, especially in front of those who disagree with their role, they worry that some will believe it proves they are incapable of the task. As a female lead pastor among a majority of male lead pastors in my fellowship, I can understand this concern. Pressure—both seen and unseen—comes with any leadership role. The lifeline comes through our consistent connection to God and drawing close to Him.

Today, Christians are sharply divided regarding the role of women. Some people believe that God created women for the sole purpose of marriage and procreation, while others believe that God created women to fulfill their individual purposes in any way that showcases the glory of God. The Old Testament leader Deborah fulfilled various roles, such as wife, mother, and judge. Her spiritual influence changed the course of history for the Jewish people. The world would not have been the same had Deborah not utilized her God-given skills both in and beyond her home.

The woman described in Proverbs 31 also used her gifts for the good of her household and her community. She managed and operated her own business (Proverbs 31:15–16). She participated in compassion ministry (v. 20). She worked from morning until night, and "her children call her blessed" (v. 28). Operating at her full potential both within and outside her home, she had won her husband's full confidence. Her capabilities and character meant that he lacked nothing of value. She was a source of good and not harm (vv. 11–12) to her family, "worth far more than rubies" (v. 10), a most valuable gemstone. The Scriptures beautifully applaud and honor a woman who makes the most of her gifts and uses her talents to glorify God and honor her loved ones.

God designed every woman with skills and abilities. Operating in those abilities should not bring harm but rather build the church and contribute to God's overall redemptive plan for humanity, no matter what the role. If a woman can best utilize her skills through leadership, then she must not hide her talents but step into her divinely assigned role.

When leaders face their fears, God begins to do things in and through their lives that are beyond our control. When that work is set in motion, there is no end to what God will do. As we learned in previous chapters through the stories of those who have gone before us, full dependence on who God is and the truth of His Word will propel a leader to greater depths of trust and joy. Relying on God means diving into the truth of his Word because it is the only thing that will keep us from drowning. God wants us to glorify Him; He chooses to make himself known to humanity through humanity. He takes our surrendered weaknesses and adds His almighty strength so that Christ Jesus is made known. In this manner, even our human frailties can become strengths when partnered with God's strength.

Let Unity Reign

Part of being courageous means not fearing the competition. Cheering other women and men on to success is crucial for united followers of Christ. The Body of Christ has no room for competitive attitudes among believers. The best leaders and team members let others shine and push people forward even when it means their own recognition and influence will be eclipsed.

Prior to my having any significant leadership role, a coworker and I were given a weighty assignment by our supervisor. I invested time outside of regular work hours to make it a success. I planned, prayed, organized, researched, and did everything within my power to make my portion a success. My coworker, however, worked under a different timeline. The night before our presentation, I discovered she had only prepared a few notes. Next to my three-ring binder and numerous page-protected notes, it seemed she had not pulled her weight on this presentation. I was surprised by her lack of organization, but I didn't want our presentation to flop, so I offered to let her use some of my notes. The next day, we shared my notes, and she stole the show. She delivered her part of the presentation brilliantly, and afterward, it seemed that people remembered her more than me.

For several weeks, I brooded over this experience. I thought I was concealing my feelings well until my boss confronted me. He was kind in his approach and sincerely concerned about why my morale seemed lower than usual. I told him that I was fine, but he was unwilling to let it go. Finally, I confessed how disappointed I was with how my portion of the presentation had gone a few weeks earlier. He told me that if I carried jealousy regarding her success, I would put a lid on my own potential for success. He advised me to let go of my jealousy and cheer her on. It didn't seem fair, but it's one of the best lessons I learned under his leadership. I did as he suggested. I confessed my jealousy to the Lord and asked for His forgiveness. After that, when someone mentioned my coworker's amazing presentation, I agreed and let God build my character a little more in that moment. It didn't matter who received more credit; the important part was that our intended message had been communicated.

One of the greatest things we can do as female leaders is to cheer on other women to success. When the world models cutthroat competition, we have an opportunity to model unity and sisterly love as followers of Christ. This is especially important to model for younger female leaders. Let's be secure enough in Christ that we can recognize and celebrate the successes and achievements of others.

What God is doing in our world is an enormous task. He is mobilizing every follower of Christ, both male and female, to make Christ known before He returns. There is plenty of room for everyone's skills to be put to good use. The work of God is too big for us to feel threatened by the talents and abilities of others. The Enemy's mission is to kill, steal, and destroy. Our greatest strategy for thwarting his plans is to unite together in the love of Christ Jesus to accomplish His purposes together. Let us be intentional about spurring one another on, even those who may not reciprocate.

Facing our fears often requires facing our enemies. This is one of the toughest parts of putting our faith into action. I learned at an early age that not everyone likes me, even if he or she seems not to have a good reason for it. As long as we are in these earthly bodies, we will have enemies—individuals who don't support or agree with what you're doing—and have let you know it. I'm not referring to those we perceive as enemies yet who have never uttered a word of opposition. When we know someone is against us, it touches a nerve deep inside us. We focus on the fact that they've judged us to be stupid, failures, or fakes. Why do such people rattle us? Why do these situations rattle us? Because somewhere deep inside, we are afraid that they might be right in their off-base assumptions.

The great news is that God is our biggest fan! He will never leave us hanging or forget what He called us to do.

He isn't swayed by others' gossip and criticism about us. He wants us to succeed in making Him known. He stands ready to give us supernatural encouragement and strength. Women in leadership can be courageous when they know that God is for them (Joshua 1:5).

How can a woman know when God is calling her to ministry and leadership? One answer cannot suffice here. Generally speaking, she'll have an initial inspired thought, followed by a time of contemplation and prayer; then the only step left is for her to take some sort of action. This is where I think many of us chicken out. We may take time to think about it, but we stop in our tracks at the first unfavorable response from someone or the first uncomfortable feeling we have. Our minds argue with our spirits until reason wins out and we shut down the idea. I've done this more than I want to admit.

Putting your faith into action takes courage and means resisting the awkward feelings that threaten your personal security. Once you take the first step and follow it through, then you can better assess the wisdom of your actions. Talking over your ideas with someone who routinely seems to take faith risks is also a good idea. He or she will have had experiences to strengthen your resolve and help keep your doubts and fears at bay.

I fully believe we are living in the last days. Because the time is short, it's imperative that everyone step up and do what God has called him or her to do. It's not acceptable to hold back because of fear or tradition. Each of us has a responsibility to follow God's calling. My husband would not allow me to stand behind him. He pushed me out in front and affirmed the gifts and skills that he saw in me. I do the same for him in his skills and calling. This is not the time to worry about traditional gender roles; we need all men and all women out in the harvest field doing their jobs so that as many people as possible can be reached with the gospel message. When Christ returns for His Bride, we ALL need to have done our part to get people ready for Him.

Here are a few practical ways to encourage women to grow in their leadership abilities:

- Cheer them on; be a fan, not a hater.
- Be honest about their strengths and weaknesses.
- Listen to their ideas and concerns.
- Offer opportunities to let them grow and shine.
- Help them discover outlets where they can use their skills.

- Introduce them to others who have similar interests or skills.
- Consider their qualifications and giftings before their gender.

Truths to Remember:

Truth—I foster unity in the Body of Christ when I set aside jealousy.

Truth—I am exactly who God created me to be.

Your Turn:

1. What specific women could you be cheering for today?

2. Describe the most recent time when your fear and your faith collided. What was the outcome?

What is another truth that describes your life right now? As you reflect on these truths (look back at chapters 1–3), may you be inspired to keep stepping out in faith!

Personal Truth 4:

Truth #5 Women in leadership are unstoppable!

"He who began a good work in you will carry it on to completion until the day of Christ Jesus." Philippians 1:6

Why Not Women?

The concept of freedom has changed dramatically for American women over the past seventy years. People no longer raise eyebrows when a woman is announced as a company president or government official. Within many church denominations, people recognize and respect women for their leadership abilities. Beth Moore, one of my favorite Bible teachers, inspires many because of her devotion to God and her desire to understand His Word. She comes from a denomination known for not allowing women to exercise authority or leadership within the church, yet she has an incredible following of both women and men. God has given her a voice in the Christian community and blessed her ministry.

Cardinal Health, one of Ohio's leading healthcare organizations, introduced an initiative called "Widen the Circle," which intentionally encourages female leadership and participation. Since its inception, the company has identified ways for women within the company to climb the corporate ladder and achieve their maximum potential. Cardinal Health is committed to including women at every level of leadership within the company. Women make up 46.9% of the U.S. labor force; however, they hold only 4.2% of CEO jobs at Fortune 500 companies and 16.6% of board seats at those organizations.[17] Recently ranked one of the top 100 companies for working mothers, Cardinal Health has taken proactive steps to widen the circle to include more female employees.[18] According to Chief Executive Officer George Bartlett, Cardinal Health is striving to create an environment "where we look great because we have great people that look and think differently."[19] Making this initiative known will undoubtedly draw women to apply for positions within the company. In addition, this will play an instrumental role in keeping female employees committed and loyal to the organization. When employees have few opportunities for growth, they may look elsewhere for employment. In many cases, employees will remain long-term with employers when they feel valued and developed. When a company believes in its employees, employees are more likely to believe in the company; this creates a situation where everyone wins.

Practically speaking, credibility and competency top the list of hiring priorities. In their book *Her Place at the Table: A Women's Guide to Negotiating Five Key Challenges to Leadership Success,* authors Deborah M. Kolb, Judith Williams, and Carol Frohlinger state that "for a woman, establishing credibility can be an uphill campaign" They also argue that although the number of women in top management positions has doubled since 1995, it's still insufficient, as women still hold less than 10 percent of the corporate officer-level positions.[20] According to the authors, this is in spite of the fact that "women equal or surpass male colleagues across a wide range of interpersonal measures—motivating groups, giving feedback, and accessibility. But they also score higher in performance measures that weigh their contribution to the bottom line."[21] As women are tested to ensure they have what it takes to lead, they must be given opportunities to practice their skills in the field. I spoke with a professional leadership coach in Dayton, Ohio, who mentioned that the women in leadership roles that she coaches receive far more scrutiny than the men she coaches. Women may have years of hard work ahead of them, but they have made significant progress. If more companies, government offices, and religious fellowships will only widen the circle, women and men in healthy competition will spur one another on to success.

Am I suggesting that the church should follow the model of the ever-shifting business world? The simple answer is, no. The Early Church modeled the concept of widening the circle when they waited for the Gift of the Holy Spirit's empowerment (Acts 1:4–8) and then lived out Joel's prophecy, that in the last days God's Spirit would be poured out on ALL flesh.

Somehow, the freedom and unity declared in time of the Early Church got hijacked in more recent history. The Church no longer resembled the Early Church and made rules and regulations specifically for women in their fellowships. Now, the Church as a whole is shifting back to the precious truth that Joel prophesied and Peter preached in Acts 2, that there are Kingdom roles for men and women, young and old— and, as Paul added, rich and poor, slave and free (Galatians 3:28). Though there was previously ample biblical evidence of women in leadership, Jesus' ministry in the New Testament and the commissioning of the Early Church blew those doors wide open!

God's work in those who follow Him never ends; the responsibility for perfecting and completing His work through human beings is His (Philippians 1:6). When people know that another person believes in them, they excel and surpass expectations. This is true not only in the professional realm but also in the way the world treats women and children. In the book, *Shaping the Future: Girls and Our Destiny*, an advocate wrote: "Today's girls are tomorrow's women, and...for a girl to reach her full potential in all stages of life, she needs to be nurtured in an empowering environment, where her needs for survival, protection, and development are met and her equal rights safeguarded."[22] This is not meant to exclude boys or men from this broader picture, but rather to recognize that too many people have viewed girls as less important than boys. However, it only makes sense, as many have suggested, that when girls and women are allowed to flourish and achieve their full potential, the lives of boys and men will also be enriched and improved.

Improving the treatment of women and girls, both worldwide and locally, will improve the environment in which people live and grow. As more women are recruited for the professional arena, as more women are elected to government positions, and as more women are allowed to serve in leadership roles in our religious fellowships, the younger generation of girls will no longer view themselves as rebels if they aspire to work and serve in positions of leadership. The ripple effect of respect for women and equality in society will increase as both young women and men observe female role models in leadership.

While this task seems overwhelming, the power of the Holy Spirit, working on behalf of believers, can bring this to fruition. On the Day of Pentecost, 3,000 people believed Peter's message and were baptized (Acts 2:41). Believers who received the infilling of the Holy Spirit did not hold superior status but simply became conduits through which the power of God could work. The Bible never claims individuals who operate in the gifts of the Spirit are superior; as a matter of fact, God loves and honors humility (1 Peter 5:6). One must never underestimate what the Holy Spirit will accomplish through willing people. Authors Nicholas D. Kristof and Sheryl WuDunn recognize the Spirits' power, as reflected in this statement: "It is particularly crucial to incorporate Pentecostalism into a movement for women's rights around the globe, because it is gaining ground more quickly than any other faith."[23] As believers recognize their biblical role in making the world a better place for all human beings, they have become a notable force behind humanitarianism and foreign aid. Around the world, Kristof and WuDunn note, "Pentecostal churches typically encourage all members of the congregation to speak up and preach during the service. So for the first time, many ordinary women find themselves exercising leadership and declaring their positions on moral and religious matters."[24]

One can readily ascertain that the principles demonstrated on the Day of Pentecost influenced the founding of the Assemblies of God (AG). From the AG's very inception, women of the fellowship played a key role in God's plan to fulfill the Great Commission by preaching the gospel message around the world. Women were ordained and served as lead pastors from the beginning of this fellowship in 1914. In a time when the world was markedly a man's world, the AG encouraged women to achieve their potential and find their place in executing the Great Commission. Although leaders within this fellowship readily embrace the scriptural precedence for women in ministry, many of its adherents have operated according to societal tradition and excluded women from serving as leaders. In the twenty-first century, however, the Assemblies of God has included more women at many levels of leadership. Currently, more women than ever hold positions as lead pastors, district presbyters, executive presbyters, and professors, and at the national and district levels.

What Will *Your* Verse Be?

In the first part of this book, I mentioned that willingness is the top qualification for those who want to lead for change and make a difference for the glory of God. Steven Furtick, pastor of Elevation Church in North Carolina says it this way: "When we want what God wants for the reasons He wants, then we become unstoppable." If you look back through biblical history, you will find this to be true. Those willing to step out in faith were the ones who changed history. What does it mean to be willing? We become willing when our faith conquers our fear and we fix our gaze on the bigger picture rather than on our ever-changing circumstances.

Our willingness mobilizes us for action. In Alcoholics Anonymous, the first step toward recovery is admitting there is a problem. A dear friend of mine, who has been sober for more than three years, learned this when she went through the AA program. My friend knew she had a problem before she admitted it, but only when she was willing to recover could the transformation begin to take place. Recovery is no cakewalk after that, but it starts the process of change. It clears the path that must be followed.

I can think of dozens of reasons why I am humbled to write this book; I could easily list all of the qualifications that I don't have. But I know without a doubt that my part is to write; God's part is to do the rest. As a woman in leadership, I feel the continual tension of obedience to God's calling, the demands of the roles I serve in, the urgency of The Great Commission, and the realistic limits of my human body. What concerns me is *not* seeing the results I am praying and hoping for. I want God to do the impossible in my community, in this nation, and around the world. I do not want the doom and gloom of the news to be the final word! I realize that we will have turbulence and trials in these last days—but we are still in the Church Age, the age of God's unconditional grace. He is not willing for any to perish without know the truth about His love for them! He wants everyone everywhere to know Him.

I have lived long enough to know that God does not always accomplish His work the way I am expecting, but I also know that there is an unseen realm in which God works. We will not fully know what He is up to until we are in eternity; then we will have access to the complete download of information. However, rest assured: God *is* actively working in the realm we can see now, as well. Life-changing and supernatural works are His usual practices. His light radiates to the darkest places, His love reaches the most disenchanted, and His power is at work all over this world today. He does the impossible through people who are willing to step out in faith and believe Him for change.

I have had one compelling prayer request since my teenage years; "Lord, keep me close to You." As a teenager, I realized that I would accomplish nothing of value without Christ. I don't even remember all of the mistakes I've made, but I do remember that overcoming them seemed like impossible mountains at the time, and I was desperate for God to help me and lead me through. I wanted to please Him in every way. I wanted to give God every part of my life. I wanted Him to do the impossible through me! I wanted to walk with God like those I had read about—Enoch, Elijah, Debra, Esther, David, Paul, Priscilla, Isaiah, and Habakkuk. I wanted to be the watchman on the wall, be used of God like the prophets who represented the voice of God to the people. I dreamed of being close to Him and wanting Him more than anything else. So, needless to say, when I fell short, I felt I was not good enough. Much to my relief, I have learned that God does not wait until we are perfect to include us in His plan. When we stumble, He helps us get back up and keep walking. He does not criticize the way we walk but offers instruction though His Word. We will hear His voice of support and be reminded of His truths when we stay close to Him. The older I get, the more I realize my desperate need for close proximity to my heavenly Father.

Staying close to God through spiritual disciplines and practices allows us opportunities to demonstrate our continual willingness. Initial willingness moves us to action, but continual willingness keeps us in active service. Human will gets in the way too quickly; it's imperative for leaders to be intentional in the time they spend in God's presence, coming away refreshed by what they've seen, experienced, and heard. Just one shift to seeing God's perspective can change everything! He holds all the answers and has all the wisdom we need. He wants to share what He knows with us so we can clearly follow Him. He may not give us word-for-word instructions, but He faithfully leads and inspires those who consult with Him. When we are willing, God opens our eyes to see what is happening around us and how we can join in the work He is doing. He calls us to the table with full knowledge of who we are and what we can contribute.

A recent TV commercial for the IPAD Air took inspiration from the Walt Whitman poem, "O Me! O Life!" It asks the question, "What will your verse be?" Let me share the poem with you:

O Me! O Life!
By Walt Whitman

"Oh me! Oh life! of the questions of these recurring,
Of the endless trains of the faithless, of cities fill'd with
the foolish,
Of myself forever reproaching myself, (for who more foolish
than I, and who more faithless?)
Of eyes that vainly crave the light, of the objects mean, of the
struggle ever renew'd,
Of the poor results of all, of the plodding and sordid crowds
I see around me,
Of the empty and useless years of the rest, with the rest me
intertwined,
The question, O me! so sad, recurring—What good amid
these, O me, O life?
Answer.
That you are here—that life exists and identity,
That the powerful play goes on, and you may con-
tribute a verse."

For Such a Time as This, Indeed.

Current world affairs and the bad news we read every day are daunting. Depression and anxiety run deep, these days. We can look around and easily wish to stay inside our shell; or, we can get outside and embrace the storm. The world news will continue to worsen; issues will continue to grow more complicated then ever. But we are here, alive at this time in history with a purpose. Best of all, God has equipped us with everything we need (Psalm 139:13).

The role models mentioned in this book are just a few of the countless women who have said yes to God's call on their lives. They spoke up, stood up, stopped looking back, moved forward, and changed the outcome of their lives and the lives of others when they followed God's leading. They were not all popular; they did not have all the answers; they did not know the outcome of their actions, but they did it anyway. They changed history—and they are no different from you and me.

You can probably think of many reasons why you should not pursue your dreams, but there are many more reasons why you should. When you step out in faith, you will change history for yourself and for those you influence. God will never leave you or forsake you. He will guide your path. He is looking for willing people to pour His presence, His glory, and His blessing into. He wants to shine through your life. Will you let Him? God's work in us is immeasurable because His work in us never ends. Only He has the power to begin it and complete it, and completing it is exactly what He promised He would do. It is on his shoulders to finish the work He started in us, to provide the opportunities for us to use our talents and skills. It is up to us to see what next step He is directing us to take and then to be willing to take it, no holding back. Recognize it, and go for it!

Remember Esther? When she felt fearful about stepping up, taking the risk, and allowing God to use her, Mordecai warned her: "If you remain silent at this time, relief and deliverance for the Jews will arise from another place, but you and your father's family will perish. And who knows but that you have come to your royal position for such a time as this?" (Esther 4:14). This was a call to battle. "If you don't stand up and fight, then we're all going to die," her cousin was telling her. "Now go do what you know is right!" This verse can be summed up by, and was perhaps the inspiration for, the phrase, "You Go Girl!"

This is not simply an inspiring historical challenge—it's a call to action and obedience! Now is the time to follow the prompting and leading of the Holy Spirit in your life. Now is the time to act without counting everything it will cost you. This is the time to make Christ known. His yoke is easy and His burden is light (Matthew 11:30).

Esther was aware of problem. Then she waited to see how God wanted her to participate in resolving the problem. Her role ended up being more than she probably imagined or wanted it to be—she was to speak up, face the one in charge, and ask for the impossible! She did not stay silent. She spoke out, and she will forever go down in history as a hero. Because she dared to use her voice, many lives were saved.

For people who are willing to follow God's leading, He promises to show them the right path, (Proverbs 3:5–6). Such people become unstoppable because God's plans are unstoppable. If you have aligned yourself with God, you have embraced Christ as the Son of God (John 14:6). Willing people are not perfect; they have not arrived at the ultimate levels of maturity. Rather, they are simply willing to follow God, regardless of the personal cost. When we desire to be a conduit for Him, to communicate His message, then we have aligned ourselves with Him; we will be His mouthpieces for this generation.

God wants to include you in His plan. Find the path He has prepared for you, and start walking! If you ever start to doubt His calling, keep in mind the truth about who you are in Him—you are His creation, His child. Why you? Why not you? God doesn't show favoritism (Ephesians 6:9). He's not looking for someone older, younger, smarter, more experienced, wealthier, or more of a man than you are to do the work to which He has called you. He's calling you. If you are willing, He will change the world through you.

Truths to Remember:

Truth—I am going to follow God's leading today.

Truth—If I remain silent then others will miss out on the message God wants to share through my life.

Your Turn:

1) What do you want?

2) What does God want to do in and through your life?

3) How well does what you want and what God wants line up?

What is another truth that describes your life right now? As you reflect on these truths (look back at chapters 1-4 and list each personal truth below), may you be inspired to keep stepping out in faith!

Personal Truth 1:

Personal Truth 2:

Personal Truth 3:

Personal Truth 4:

Personal Truth 5:

My prayer for you is that you will connect with the God of this Universe—that through Him, you will know what He wants you to do for His Kingdom. I pray that you will not be sidetracked by all of he reasons why you can't or couldn't, but that, instead, you will release control of what you have to God—who you are, your skills and talents—so that you may see what God can do with what you have. With Him, you too can be unstoppable!

> *"To him who is able to do immeasurably more than all we ask or imagine, according to his power that is at work within us, to him be glory" (Ephesians 3:20).*

End Notes

1. Carole E. Becker, *Leading Women: How Church Women Can Avoid Leadership Traps and Negotiate the Gender Maze* (Nashville, TN: Abingdon Press, 1996), 23.

2. Tabitha Yeatts, *Joan of Arc: Heavenly Warrior* (New York, NY: Sterling, 2009), 3.

3. Jay Williams, *Joan of Arc: Warrior Saint* (New York, NY: Sterling 1963), 11.

4. Ibid., 102.

5. Ibid.

6. Elizabeth Cody Kimmel, *Ladies First: Daring American Women Who Were Second to None* (Washington DC: National Geographic Society, 2006), 85.

7. Ibid. p.85

8. Ibid, 100.

9. Anne Beiler, *Twist of Faith: The Story of Anne Beiler, the Founder of Auntie Anne's Pretzels* (Nashville, TN: Thomas Nelson Publishing, 2008), Kindle location 2502.

10. Carole E. Becker, *Leading Women: How Church Women Can Avoid Leadership Traps and Negotiate the Gender Maze* (Nashville, TN: Abingdon Press, 1996), 22.

11. Hoppin, 83.

12. Ruth Hoppin, *Priscilla's Letter: Finding the Author to the Epistle to the Hebrews* (Fort Bragg, CA: Lost Coast Press, 1997), 85.

13. Gill and Cavaness, 114.

14. Ibid.

15. Ibid., 81.

16. William J. Webb, *Slaves, Women, and Homosexuals: Exploring the Hermeneutic of Cultural Analysis* (Downers Grove, IL: InterVarsity Press, 2001), Kindle location 3111.

17. Julanne Hohbach, "Shattering the Ceiling," *Columbus CEO* (April 2013), 20.

18. Ibid.

19. Ibid., 21.

20. Deborah M. Kolb, Judith Williams, Carol Frohlinger, *Her Place at the Table: A Women's Guide to Negotiating Five*

Key Challenges to Leadership Success (San Francisco, CA: Jossey-Bass, 2004), 11.

21. Ibid.

22. Phyllis Kilbourne, ed. *Shaping the Future: Girls and Our Destiny* (Pasadena, CA: William Carey Library, 2008), 10.

23. Nicholas D. Kristof and Sheryl WuDunn, *Half the Sky: Turning Oppression into Opportunity for Women Worldwide* (New York, NY: Vintage Books, 2009), 143.

24. Ibid.

About the Author

Kelly Preston is the lead pastor of Eastside Community Church, in Columbus Ohio. She is an ordained minister with the Assemblies of God, and has a Master's degree in Christian Ministries. Kelly is passionate about leading people towards their God-given potential.

Kelly has been teaching and preaching for over 15 years. She also served as an Assemblies of God World Missionary in North Africa and the Middle East, as an overseas missionary, she worked with and counseled people from various cultures and countries. Today she pastors a church of "Ordinary people who are serving an extraordinary God!"

Kelly and her husband, Greg, love life and love raising their 3 children. Kelly loves being with her family, drinking coffee, running, and reading.

One of her life verses includes: Zephaniah 3:17… *"The Lord your God is with you, He is mighty to save. He will take great delight in you, He will quiet you with His love, He will rejoice over you with dancing."*

You can find more information about Kelly and the ministry of Eastside Community Church at www.eccag.org.

CPSIA information can be obtained at www.ICGtesting.com
Printed in the USA
BVOW03s2107081214

R6057200001B/R60572PG377820BVX1B/1/P